To Na...
Enjoy!
Susan R. Jones ♡
5-9-03

Susan R. Jones
3536 N 400 E
Danville, IN 46122
317-892-4712

The Unexpected Adventures of
Catherine Genevieve

by Susan R Jones

Dedicated to:

Catherine's Grandsons

Bryan   Brad   Bernie   Jeff   Jon   Eric

and Great Grandchildren and all future babies

Samantha

Justin Coleman

Carissa Coleman

Jon M.

Amelia Jones

Riley

Mackenzie

(Gavin)

Catherine

Jewelry Photographer
L B Photo

Collage Photographer
Jeri Bunting

Jewelry Designs by
Susan R. Jones
© 1998 Vintage Pin Studio

First, Let's Meet Catherine Genevieve

O n a warm spring day in 1911, Catherine Genevieve Wolfe was born. Her clear blue eyes were full of promise and hope as she began her life on a little farm nestled in the velvet rolling hills of Southern Indiana.

The nation was marching, full steam, into the twentieth century. Wm. H. Taft was the President. Immigrants were streaming into Ellis Island at a record rate of over 11,000 per day, hoping for a better life in America. Thousands paraded down 5th Avenue in New York City, demanding that women get the right to vote. The Chevrolet Motor Company was incorporated. Crisco was invented and Domino Sugar was introduced. Gold was discovered in Indian Creek, Alaska. Air conditioning was invented, and the first Indianapolis 500 Mile Race was run.

In New York, the Ziegfeld Follies were featuring Irving Berlin's "Everybody Does It", and Helen Hayes appeared on Broadway.

Coca-Cola cost 5 cents. A bicycle was $11.95,

and an Acme lawn mower was $5.89.
Yes, our lives are quite different today than
in Catherine Genevieve's day. Each
generation pushes itself to reach for more
knowledge and to attain a better lifestyle
for their families. People who have a
passion for life will always be busy...this is
as it should be.

As you enjoy this trip to yesterday, through
the memories of Catherine Genevieve,
think about your family, past and present.
Then take a little time to write down a
memory or tell a story. Make that phone
call or write a note. Hug those little ones
every chance you get, and bake (or buy) a
few extra cookies... you never know when
someone may stop by.

HIGH WATER!

Catherine Genevieve sat up straight in the back seat of the family carriage. She dreamily smoothed her Sunday dress and swung her legs that did not yet reach the floorboard. The sleek, brown buggy horse clip-clopped along the familiar road home from church. His hooves had a different sound on the wet ground

than on dry ground...more of a slap-slap. Hooves on dry, dusty ground had a soft thud-thud sound. Her family's carriage was shiny black with leather seats...one in the front for Pa and Ma and baby brother and one in back for Catherine Genevieve and her big brother. There was a top on the carriage, thank goodness, for the little spring shower of that morning had turned into a real "gully washer", as Pa called it! Even with the top, the family was still getting wet. Some of the fancy carriages had sides that you could roll right down, in case there was a change in the weather! Ma always carried lap quilts, and Catherine Genevieve pulled hers around her and watched the rain. Pa sat tall and handsome, with his white Sunday straw hat atop his head. Ma sat quietly, holding little brother. She was gentle and soft spoken... her pretty brown hair was rolled up in a bun, under her Sunday hat. She wore a dainty brooch at her neck...the one she had worn when she used to teach school. Catherine Genevieve loved it when Ma read stories and poems to them.

The buggy horse didn't seem to mind the rain. In fact, Catherine Genevieve would love to have gotten out of her good clothes and run through the puddles with her bare feet. Her straw hat, with its yellow ribbons, itched her head full of blond curls, her petticoats were hot and sweaty, and her little toes longed to be free of the leather shoes! Catherine Genevieve did love going to church. It was nearly the only time she saw her friends, for their family farm was far out in the countryside. This was many, many years ago, and Catherine Genevieve's home was different in many ways from your home, today. For instance,

Remember that thou
keep holy the Sabbath-day.

Christmas card from Catherine's aunt Buelah,
Dec. 22, 1909

there was no electricity. It was not yet
available in rural areas. Many things we use
every day had not yet been invented, such as
television, computers, video games, ball
point pens, magic markers, color movies,
video cameras, microwave ovens, automatic
washers and dryers, cellular phones or

playdoh, just to name a few!

Ma cooked all their food on a big stove that was heated with wood or coal. She washed all the family's clothing in big tubs, scrubbing them on a wash board. Then she hung them on a line outside in the sunshine to dry. In the winter, she hung the line across the kitchen. As the clothing dried, the fragrance of Ma's homemade soap filled the air. Pa did all the farm work with the help of two big brown mules. They pulled the plow, the planter, the cultivator, the wagon, the mower and, working together, they operated the little farm, which produced corn, wheat and oats. Pa took good care of the mules. He fed and watered them, even before he ate his own breakfast. After a hard day's work, Pa rubbed them down with a soft brush and put them in the barn with a fresh stack of alfalfa hay and a scoop of oats.

Clippity-clop, on they rode, with Catherine

Genevieve's tight yellow curls bouncing. Just around the corner would be the little, shallow creek. They would cross that, which was fun, then she would be able to see their white house. She would hurry in and change her good clothes, and maybe Pa would let her help brush the buggy horse while Ma fixed Sunday dinner. She could just smell that fried chicken, now! Then, suddenly, the carriage stopped with a jerk! The horse whinnied and moved nervously, not knowing what to do. Catherine Genevieve stood up on her tip toes and looked over Ma's shoulder to see what was wrong.

Oh my! Something QUITE UNEXPECTED had happened! The usually serene little creek was full of water. It had overflowed its banks. Catherine Genevieve and her brother stood quietly watching, so as not to bother Pa. They knew he would know what to do. Pa always knew what to do. He looked the situation over, told everyone to hang on, and he urged the buggy horse on. The buggy horse seemed to understand that Pa would not ask him to do anything that was not safe, so he cautiously stepped into the swollen, moving water.

Catherine Genevieve had never seen the

water so high. She hung on to the back of
Ma's seat and bit her lip to keep from
crying. Pa talked easy to the buggy horse
as they went deeper into the water.
Catherine Genevieve felt something on
her feet. She looked down, and water was
coming onto the floorboard! Catherine
Genevieve made a QUICK DECISION
to jump up onto the seat. Brother jumped
up, too. They sat on the back of the buggy
with their feet on the leather seat. Soon,
they were safely across! Pa stopped the
buggy to see if everyone was all right. He
pushed his hat back on his head and smiled
as he patted the buggy horse. Everyone
laughed with relief and agreed that the
buggy horse would get a bucket of oats as
soon as they got home!

Just then, the rain stopped, and the sun
broke through the clouds. Catherine
Genevieve took a deep breath, leaned back
against the leather seat and closed her
eyes. She breathed in the sweet smell of
the earth , and she felt the warm spring air
on her face. She smiled, for she knew it
was going to be a good day, after all!

WANT TO KNOW MORE?

Would you like to know how old Catherine Genevieve was in this story?
Would you like to know the town where she went to church?
Why did Catherine Genevieve call their horse, the buggy horse?

TURN TO PAGE 29

UP UP AND AWAY!

Catherine Genevieve, with her clear blue eyes and curly blond hair...not just ordinary curly hair...I mean REALLY curly... stood in her front yard, her little hand wiping her forehead, pushing those tight curls out of her eyes. Her pretty hair was the envy of many girls, although it was a constant challenge to Catherine Genevieve.

Their little farm was far in the country, which suited Catherine Genevieve just fine, for there were new adventures every day! On this particular day, the sun was hot over head. It was late summertime in Indiana, and it was humid...sultry, as Ma called it. The sky seemed distant and so peaceful. The beauty of nature was reassuring to Catherine Genevieve. As she leaned back against the sugar maple tree, she knew for sure there was a God, for no one else could have created anything so splendid. Along came a slight breeze, and with it was carried the fragrance of the new mown hay. Every country child remembers, forever, that sweet, unmistakable smell.

Catherine Genevieve could hear Ma in the kitchen, still cleaning up from the big

noon time dinner. She loved it when it was hay season because there were extra men and older boys helping. That meant a big, wonderful noon dinner, just like Sunday, only better! That day, they had a pork roast, mashed potatoes, green beans with bacon chunks ,and 3 apple pies. Pa liked a slice of sharp cheese on his apple pie. Oh, best of all were the buttermilk biscuits Ma mixed up in a big blue crockery bowl. She would sprinkle flour on the kitchen table and roll out the soft dough with the wooden rolling pin she had gotten for a wedding present. Then, Catherine Genevieve would reach up high in the cabinet and get a glass and use it to cut out the biscuits, making circles all over the dough. Ma would put them on a flat pan and into the

hot oven. They were the best, ever, with home churned butter and raspberry jam.

Catherine Genevieve's family was growing. Now, besides her 2 brothers, she had a little sister, and when there was a lot of "company" for dinner, they got to eat at a little wooden table on the back porch. This was a real treat, because they didn't have to be so quiet or watch their manners too much!

Catherine Genevieve's attention was drawn to the barn, where she could see the men bringing up another load of hay. She scampered off, with her brothers, to watch the excitement! They were putting the hay from the field into the barn to store it. Here's how it worked. There was a door at the top of the barn which opened into the hay loft. The hay was lifted up to the hay loft by a rope and pully

system which was attached just outside the door. When the hay was attached by a hook to one end of the rope, then a horse or mule would walk, with the other end of the rope attached to its harness, thus pulling the hay up, up, to the hay loft. A helper in the loft would stack it where it would be stored, safe and dry. The horses, mules, cows and goats would eat the hay all winter when there was no clover or alfalfa growing in the pasture.

Catherine Genevieve's farm used hay for feeding the animals and straw was used for bedding for the animals. She thought it was funny that some of the town children didn't know the difference between hay and straw. One time, her friend from town was trying to get their mule to eat a handful of straw! Here is the difference. Hay comes from a field full of clover and alfalfa, sweet plants that the animals love and must have to be healthy. All summer, the animals eat these plants outside in the pasture, but, in Indiana, they do not grow in the winter. So, in the summertime, the farmers cut some of the rich pasture with a mower. They let it lay to dry in the hot sun. They turn it over with a rake, to dry the other side. Then, after 2 or 3 days, they begin to gather it into bundles and store it in the hayloft for the winter. Now, straw, on the other hand, is used for bedding for the animals to lie on. Straw is a by-product of the oat and wheat harvest. When these grains are harvested, only the top of the plant, which contains the grains, is cut. This leaves the bottom of the plant, now called "stubble" standing in the field. The farmer then cuts the "stubble" with a mower and gathers it up to use all year. Straw has very little nutrition and is much lighter in color and weight than hay. In Catherine Genevieve's day, the field equipment was, of course, pulled by horses or mules. Today, you will see huge tractors pulling mowers and hay balers, which form the hay and straw into neat bales, all tied with string or wire. Even with all the modern equipment, though, making hay or straw is a very hot job!

All too soon, the excitement was over. While the men pumped drinks of cold water from the outside pump, the young boys took off their hats and splashed water on their sweaty heads. The big brown mules drank their fill before they all headed back through the field to gather up the last load.

Catherine Genevieve's brothers began playing with the ropes, pulling them up and down. Then they hooked the handle of a big metal bucket on the end of the rope... the big bushel bucket they used to carry

feed to the cow. Let's put something in it, they said, looking around. Then they looked at Catherine Genevieve... she was just the right size! She made a QUICK DECISION! In the bucket she hopped . She scrunched down, ready for a new adventure! Her brothers pulled the other end of the rope and up, up and away went Catherine Genevieve. Oh, it was so much fun...just like a ride at the county fair! She leaned over to look down , and something QUITE UNEXPECTED happened! The bucket began to swing back and forth. She was high in the air. She could see the door to the hayloft. The bucket was swaying back and forth, back and forth, back and forth. Catherine Genevieve began to feel dizzy. She tried to scream, but all that would come out was a little whisper. She could see her brothers hanging on tightly to the rope. They began to slowly let her down. Soon she was safely on the ground. They all had a feeling they had done a dangerous thing, and they never repeated that adventure again!

After that day, Catherine Genevieve had a fear of tight places and heights, and she never rode another ride at the county fair...

Ma and Pa always wondered why.....

WANT TO KNOW MORE?

Would you like to know the names of Pa's mules?
Would you like to know where this farm was located?
Would you like to know where the big bucket came from?

TURN TO PAGE 39

Catherine ordered her hat from this post card ad

WINDOW SHOPPING

Catherine Genevieve was so excited this sunny summer morning! Her family was going to the city! Her Pa had business there, and Ma was smiling at the thought of buying some new fabrics for sewing. There were so many chores to do on the farm, and all the work had to be done before they could leave.

This was long, long ago, and when you went to the city, you dressed "properly". Pa and the boys had on their "Sunday" clothes. Overalls were just for working on the farm and, sometimes, for school. Ladies and girls, of course, always wore dresses. Today, Catherine Genevieve chose her nice crisp blue school dress with the white collar and the red bow at the neck. She wore the hat that she had ordered from New York City.

Her curly hair had now turned a soft brown with auburn highlights. She was growing up and had begun to spend a lot of time in front of the mirror, trying to control her hair, but it proved to have a mind of its own, much like Catherine Genevieve!

Going to the city was such an adventure... and a long trip. There were no interstates or smooth highways and no fast food

places along the way to have a kids meal or use the restrooms! Ma always packed a basket with fruit and cookies to "tide them over". Before Pa had the truck, he had to drive the horse and carriage when he had business in the city. He would have to stay overnight, so the rest of the family did not go. It would have been too difficult and too expensive to find a place for all to stay. The convenient, lovely hotels and motels, with the pools and saunas, the game rooms, comfortable beds and those cute little soaps and shampoos were not yet available in Catherine Genevieve's day!

So off they went...Pa and Ma in the front seat, with new baby brother. This was baby brother's first summer. All the older children sat in the back of the truck on a quilt Ma had spread out. Little sister sat primly on the patchwork, her soft curls peeking out from the sides of her hat. Catherine Genevieve couldn't help but smile when she remembered little sister's predicament the night before. It was dark, and the wind was blowing hard. Little sister had to run out to the outhouse, which is an outside bathroom. Most homes at that time did not have inside bathrooms. Well, Pa had been patching a roof leak earlier that day, with tar. He had left the bucket of tar sitting outside, and the strong wind had blown the bucket over, spilling the tar. The black, sticky tar ozzed over the path that led to the outhouse. Little sister, in her long white nightgown and bare little feet, stepped right in the gooey tar...with both feet! Ma had to scrub and scrub to get all the tar off!

Yes, children could ride in the back of a truck, back then. There were no seatbelts and hardly any traffic. The roads were dirt and gravel until they got nearly to the city. Pa drove about 15 miles an hour, and that was pretty fast! Since the children were in the back of the truck, what would they do if they needed something? Well, Ma had rigged up a special way for them to signal her and Pa. First, Ma tied a heavy string to the windshield wiper. Then she put the string over the cab of the truck and tied it on to the back of the truck, where the children were sitting. Then, if anyone needed help, they were to tug on the string, which would wiggle the windshield wiper. Pa and Ma would see it, and Pa would stop. That was quite a good system, don't you think?

The trip went well. The city was busy and bright and noisy. It was bustling with crowds of people and cars and trucks and a few horses and buggies. The streets were

so crowded that a policeman had to stand in the middle of the street, and hold a sign that said STOP on one side and GO on the other! They sure didn't need a sign like that in Catherine Genevieve's little town! Pa got his business done. Ma got several yards of pretty calico fabric, and everyone got to eat in a restaurant.

Catherine Genevieve was somewhat enchanted by the spell of the big city. The fashionable clothing on display in the store windows stirred a desire in her. She looked forward to the day she and her sister were old enough to go to the city by themselves. They would spend the whole day shopping in the big department stores. They would begin at the top floor, look at all the dresses and the coats with fur collars...then they would go to the main floor and sample all the fancy perfumes from Paris and New York...then work their way clear down to the bargain basement! They would drop a nickel in the dispenser by the door and take a big shopping bag to carry all their purchases. When they were so tired they could not walk another step, they would stop at the lunch counter, sit on a spinning stool and order a cherry Coke, for a nickel...if they had a nickel left! They would laugh and talk about the bargains they had found.

Catherine Genevieve looked in each store window as Pa drove slowly toward the edge of the city. Then, suddenly, there it  was...the most beautiful dress she had ever seen in the whole wide world! She wanted a closer look. She made a QUICK DECISION to pull the emergency string. She tugged on the string, and Pa stopped. Catherine Genevieve hopped from the back of the truck and ran to the store window. The dress was robin egg blue, her favorite color. She could just see herself wearing that dress to church or to the opening school program.. Maybe she could remember all the details, and Ma could sew her one just like it. With one last look at the neckline and how the waist dropped, she turned to go back to the truck. Oh, no... something QUITE UNEXPECTED had happened! The truck was gone. Catherine Genevieve looked quickly down the street. There went Pa's truck, with her little sister and her brothers all waving their arms.

All adoring visions of herself in the dress quickly gave way to sheer panic! She ran down the sidewalk as fast as her country legs would carry her. After what seemed like a very long time, Pa stopped the truck. Her brothers and sister were yelling and pulling on the emergency string. Catherine Genevieve came running, breathlessly, toward the truck. Pa and Ma got out to see what all the fuss was about. Catherine Genevieve quickly explained how she had pulled the string so that she could go look at the most beautiful dress in the world in that store window back there and when she pulled the string Pa had stopped so she got out to look and then she looked up and Pa had run off an left her so she ran as fast as she could and thank goodness Pa had stopped because she guessed that if he hadn't she would have had to run all the way home!! Catherine Genevieve took a deep breath. Pa and Ma began to laugh. Then all the other children began to laugh. Pa said he guessed the emergency string didn't work, for the reason he had stopped, back there, was for a stop sign. Everyone was still laughing...everyone, that is, except Catherine Genevieve! She wasted no time climbing back into the truck.

Ma brought out the basket of oatmeal cookies and apples and passed them out.

As Pa started driving, the other children began eating their cookies, so the laughter quieted.

Catherine Genevieve, having regained her dignity, dreamily watched the city, as it slowly disappeared from sight. She was carefully remembering every detail of ...the dress.........

WANT TO KNOW MORE?

Where did Catherine Genevieve live?
What year was it?
Do you know who was President, then?

TURN TO PAGE 49

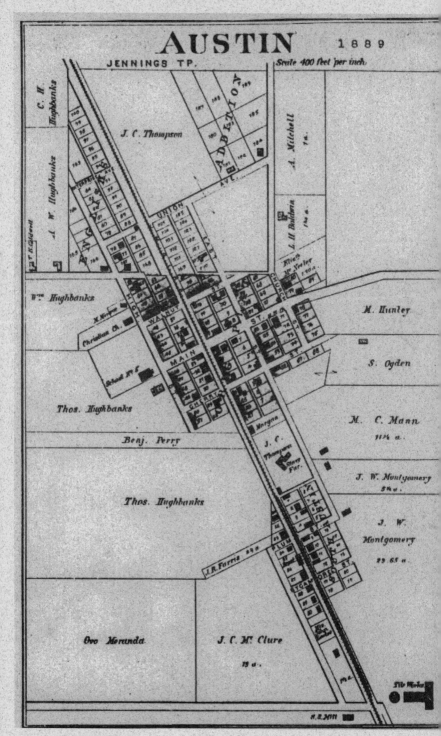

AUSTIN

1889

JENNINGS TP.

Scale 400 feet per inch

HIGH WATER...
IN RETROSPECT

The year was 1915. Catherine Genevieve was just 4 years old. Woodrow Wilson was President of the United States. Due to several complex political causes, World War I had begun, marked by a single act... the assination of Archduke Ferdinand and his wife, Sophie, in Austria. War was raging through Europe, and soon the U.S. would be involved. American "doughboys", as our soldiers were called, would be marching to the singing of George M. Cohan's "Over There". It was a difficult time for Catherine's young parents, I am sure. It was an uncertain time, and yet they had a great faith in God and in their country. So, they all worked together.

This story took place in Scott County,

located in the Southeastern part of Indiana, with Scottsburg as the county seat. Catherine's parents, Verne and Ethel Wolfe had purchased a small farm just outside Austin, in Jennings Township in 1907.

The town of Austin has a rich history with far reaching roots. Recently, Catherine (my mother) and I took a drive to Austin to do a bit of research for this book. Catherine was remembering the crossroads town of 1915, so, needless to say, we were pleasantly surprised to drive into a lovely, prospering town of the 1990's! We quickly found the Methodist Church, which

Austin Methodist Church

Catherine's family had attended.

According to records I found, it is the oldest church in Austin, built in 1859. Soon, we were at the Austin Public Library, a beautiful branch of the Scott County Public Library. The friendly, knowledge-able staff soon made us feel very welcome! It was evident that Jennings Township has a deep seated and proud past.

Austin's far reaching roots began in Austin, Texas, according to Dr. Bogardus (1906-1992), a prominent Austin physician. Austin was named for Austin, Texas by a number of v terans of the Mexican War, who had been given land in Scott County as a reward for their service. The veterans had been stationed in Austin, Texas...so they named their new home in Indiana, Austin, according to an article by George Yater in the Louisville Times.

The beginnings of the town were tied to the opening of the railroad from Jeffersonville to Indianapolis, which is now part of the Pennsylvania Railroad System. Timbering was one of the most important enterprises in the latter part of the 19th century. There were saw mills supplying lumber for many businesses in town. Oak timber, prized for steamboat building, was sent to New Albany, Jeffersonville and Madison.

Now, much of the land that was cleared by timbering grows tomatoes and corn for the chief industry of today, canning. The Morgan Packing Co. is the largest family owned plant in the U.S., according to information I found.

The town of Austin has grown from 225 people in 1890 to over 5000 in the 1990's, due to careful planning and many new businesses.

Catherine remembers the interurban, which ran from Louisville to Indianapolis, going directly through Austin. It was this inter-urban that would bring her grandparents to visit from Noblesville and Anderson. It was this interurban that carried Catherine to her new home, when she left Austin at the age of 5.

Since Catherine was so young when she lived in Austin, she could not pinpoint the exact location of their farm. There were two neighbors she remembers...Mr. and Mrs. Bartle. Mrs. Bartle's name was Carrie, and they had a daughter named Bernice. She also fondly remembers Mr. and Mrs. Billy Smith.

Catherine recalls a family trip to Madison and riding across the Ohio River on a ferry boat. The long trip was made in their carriage, pulled by their faithful "buggy" horse. This horse was a small horse, and he was kept especially for pulling the family carriage, which was a 2 seated buggy. Sometimes the children rode the buggy horse.

Catherine's family, on her mother's side, came from Amsterdam, Holland in 1650 and settled in a Dutch village in New York City. They followed their trade of merchandising, later relocating further and further West, owning mills and getting into farming. Thanks to much research by Catherine's cousin, Ruby, we can benefit from and enjoy a detailed history.

Here is an interesting account of a few days entries in the journal of James Roudebush (1821-1885) as he traveled from the New England area to find land to purchase. James was Catherine's Great-Grandfather. JOURNAL DATED MARCH 14, 1845: "This day we went to Noblesville. Noblesville is situated on a beautiful piece of ground with about one hundred and fifty houses with 5 or 6 stores and 2 or 3 taverns. This day it was cold and snowy enough. JOURNAL DATED MARCH 17, 1845 : "This day we went to see a piece of land that was for sale. The land is rolling and beautiful and lays within 5 miles of the County Seat of Hamilton County." JOURNAL DATED MARCH 30, 1845: "This day I am in company with Christian Stern. We set out for

Indianapolis or to Mr. Webb's 8 miles below. We went down on the East side of the river. The country through which we went was somewhat broken and hilly, but the scenery was beautiful. The peach trees were in bloom and the apple trees were green with leaves.. This day we got to the noted place, Indianapolis, the capital of the state. It is a large and flourishing city. The streets are broad and clean.

The State House is the most splendid building and is said to be the best State House in the Union."

Original Roudebush farm home

The land that James Roudebush purchased from Mr. Webb cost $2.25 an acre, and is located on old SR 32. One of James' sons was George Washington Roudebush (1853-1949). George was Catherine's grandfather. When George was a young boy, he told of seeing Abraham Lincoln as his campaign train stopped in Noblesville. Young George ran to see what was going on. He stood and watched as Abraham Lincoln came out onto the back of the train and stood talking to the crowd of people. He was wearing a black suit and a black hat, and the railing of the train was draped with red white and blue bunting.

George Roudebush married Laura Jones, and they had 9 children; Beula, Bertha, Ethel, Eva, Elbert, Iven, Kate, Victor and Fred. After the death of Laura, George married Amanda (Mandy) Peck.

Ethel (1880-1968) was Catherine's mother.

The Victorian home at the corner of Hannibal and 11th street in Noblesville, where Catherine's Grandparents lived after retiring from farming

Catherine's father's side of the family came to this area from Pennsylvania. Icitia (DeHaven) Wolfe (1811-1911) lived in Madison County, northeast of Lapel. One of her children was William Wolfe. He was a Whig, then a Republican, having cast his first ballot for Abraham Lincoln. He married Isabell Guinn, and they had 7 children; Viola, Sarah Avaline, James, William (called Reed), Florence, Charles, who both died young, and Verne, the youngest. Verne(1883-1958) was Catherine's father.

Catherine's mother, Ethel, attended Valparaiso University and was a teacher before her marriage. As was the regulation of the day, she gave up her teaching when she and Verne were married, to become a full time homemaker. In that day, it certainly would have been full time! They arrived in Austin, Indiana in 1907. While there,

Catherine and brother Ledner, about 1914

their first son, Glen Ledner was born, in 1909. Then in 1911 Catherine Genevieve came along, and in 1914, their third child, Robert William joined the family.

When Catherine arrived, each of her parents wanted their daughter to be named after their grandmothers. Verne's grandmother was Icitia. Ethel's grandmother was Catherine... you can see who won! Now Catherine also has a namesake, her

Catherine's grandmother Catherine

Catherine's grandmother Icitia

great granddaughter, Riley Catherine Jones! As we continued our road trip through Catherine's past, we stopped at the Dairy Bar and enjoyed a hot, tasty sandwich and fries, served up with the ease and

friendliness you seem to always find in a small town. We passed the thriving packing plants, the small businesses, the churches, schools, pre-schools and street after street of charming, well kept homes, with architecture ranging from the late 1800's to present day. We eased Mother's station wagon up Main Street past the Austin 5 & 10, a little slice of history in itself.

Austin 5 & 10

I am sure the residents of Austin appreciate just how fortunate they are to have all the conveniences of the 1990's and, yet, still retain that close hometown feeling. As we set our course toward home, I commented to Catherine that her little crossroads town had certainly changed since she left, 80 years ago. She said , yes, the town has changed just about as much as the nearly 6 year old girl who left...and the 86 year old lady who returned....

HISTORY OF UP, UP AND AWAY....

The year was around 1919. Catherine Genevieve's family now lived in Hendricks County, in the central part of Indiana, about midway between New Winchester, which is in Marion Township and North Salem, which is in Eel River Township. Danville is the county seat of Hendricks county. Their farm was located on today's C.R. 350 N., about 1/2 mile off S.R. 75. This was the second farm her family had lived on since their move to Hendricks County, so we are going to back up a bit and enjoy some history of their first move from Austin, Indiana in 1916 when Catherine was 5 years old.

Catherine remembers well that day they moved from Austin , Indiana, the only home she had ever known... it was the winter of 1916. Her father, Verne, had taken all the household furniture in the wagon, pulled by their two mules, Jack and Kate. It was a long trip from Austin to New Winchester. Her mother, Ethel, had packed all the clothing and small items into trunks and boxes. After giving her father a couple days head start, a neighbor took Catherine, her brothers, Ledner and Robert and their mother

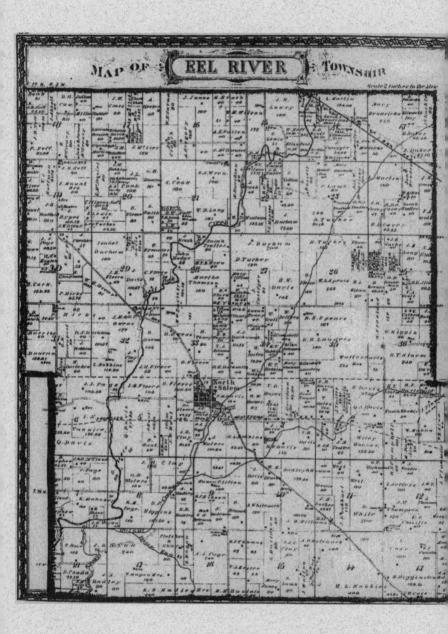

Map of **EEL RIVER** Township

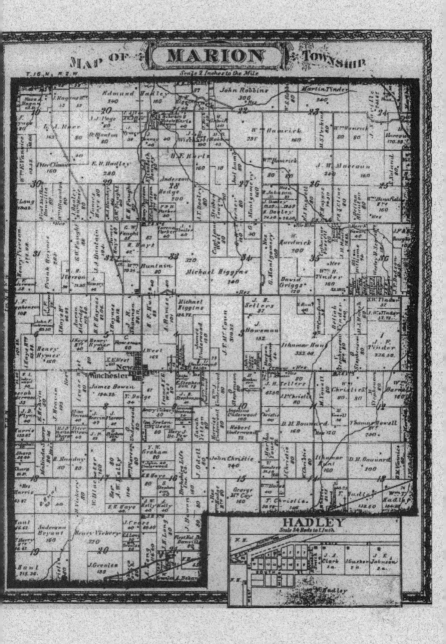

Map of MARION Township

41

to the interurban station in Austin. They
boarded the little car, which would carry
them to their new home. An interurban
was much like a train... running on tracks.
However, it was small and was designed
to carry people short distances, stopping at
each small town along the way. Catherine
remembers holding her little doll and watching the countryside, wondering what their
new home would be like. Her father was
waiting for them at the nearest station,
Coatesville, with the wagon. He excitedly
told them about their new farm. The old
log house would have to do until spring..
then he would build them a new home. He
told about the beautiful, rolling ground and
the modern towns nearby and the new
school where Ledner and Catherine would
be going. It was nearly dark when they
arrived at the farm. Catherine remembers,
well, that a neighbor, Mrs. Poer, came to
greet them. She brought a big dish of
butter beans, hot and ready to eat! It was a
much appreciated "welcome" for a weary
young family in a strange new place.

This 40 acre farm was located in Marion
Township, on today's S.R. 75, about 1 mile
or so south of New Winchester. The next
spring, her father replaced the log house
with a new home, complete with a basement. He used a slip scoop and a mule to

Catherine's New Winchester home.

pull up the dirt, one scoop at a time. This is hard to imagine when we see the excavating equipment of today! The house was very well constructed, for it still stands today. It remains a lovely country place.

Here's an interesting note. Nellie Page, a good friend to Catherine, and a lifelong resident of Hendricks County, lived in that same home as a teenager. Nellie remembers the old telephone exchange in the quaint little building which is still standing on the northwest corner of S.R. 75 and U.S. 36. It was operated by Billy Buchanan. He was the uncle of Alton Page, who was to become Nellie's husband. Now, their new home, even though it was quite modern for the time, had no electricity, for it was not yet available in rural areas. Catherine's mother had to preserve all the meat, since there was no refrigerator! She canned beef, and she sugar cured hams and bacon from the home butchered hogs. Also, she placed steaks in a big stone jar, layering them with salt and sugar. These would keep quite a while, and Catherine says they were delicious! As far as milk went, it did not have a chance to spoil. They had a cow to provide milk for the family. Her mother used the milk for all to drink, plus churning butter and cooking. If there was any left over, she let it set and turn into buttermilk, which Catherine's father considered a real treat.

Catherine also recalls when the news came that World War 1 had ended. There

was a spontaneous celebration in New Winchester, as there was in towns and cities all across the nation, I am sure. She, along with her father and brother, Ledner walked along the gravel road into town. Everyone brought pan lids, wooden spoons, American flags, musical instruments, and noisemakers of any kind. There were speeches and stories of war and of the bravery of their young men and prayers of thankfulness that it was finally over. What had seemed to be only dreams for the future were now possibilities!

Ledner, baby Laurabel, mother Ethel, Robert and Catherine, 1918

Catherine's family was growing. Now, in addition to older brother, Ledner and younger brother, Robert, Catherine had a new little sister, Laurabel, born in 1918..

Laurabel and Catherine

The two sisters were surely destined to be life long friends!

Catherine attended the big brick New Winchester school for 12 years, graduating

New Winchester School in the early 1900's

in 1929. Two of the neighbors that Catherine went to school with were John Church and Sally Joseph. These two later married and were the parents of Phyllis Merritt, who teaches at Pittsboro Elementary School. "Mrs. Merritt" has taught some of Catherine's grandchildren and great grandchildren!

The New Winchester School had been built in 1908 and served the children of the community until 1963. It was demolished a few years later. Catherine has pieces of slate, a desk and a chair which she purchased to keep as memories of happy times. The youth of this area are now incorporated into the Danville school district. Catherine also has fond memories of Pefley's Store, on the southeast corner of U.S. 36 and S.R. 75. A nickel would buy a real treat, back then!

New Winchester Baptist Church

Her family attended the lovely Baptist Church, which stands on S.R. 36. The Alumni Banquet for New Winchester school has been held in this building for several years.

The tranquil rolling countryside in the New Winchester area is dotted with cattle and grain farms and many stately 19th century homes serving as reminders of yesterday. Catherine lived in this location until she was in the third grade, 1919. That brings us to the home where the UP, UP and AWAY adventure took place. Her father purchased a farm on Co. Rd. 350 N., just east of St. Rd. 75, as stated in the beginning paragraph of this history.

Catherine lived in this home until she graduated from high school and enjoyed many, many adventures with family, friends, and neighbors. You will be treated to many of those memories in the history of the next story. Here's a bit of trivia. The "bucket" that Catherine's brothers used to give her the exciting ride was from the war. These buckets were used to carry feed for the army horses. After the war, many farmers bought them at army surplus sales to use on their farms.

The barn where the "Up, Up and Away" story took place.

Remember the blue crockery bowl and the wooden rolling pin that Catherine's mother used to roll out those tasty biscuits? Those items are proudly displayed in my kitchen. Well, time is marching on...let's move on to the next adventure!

LOOKING INTO WINDOW SHOPPING

The twentieth century was in full swing. The year was 1924. Calvin Coolidge was the president.. Catherine was 14. Her family lived in the North Salem area, on today's Co. Rd. 350 N., just off S.R. 75 in Hendricks County.

In preparation for writing this book, I drove Catherine, my mother, on a road trip to

Catherine and her youngest brother Don, around 1930.

yesterday through beautiful Eel River and Marion Townships. I had pulled off the road to write, as Mother was pointing out old neighbors' homes. We were on Co. Rd. 625 W., heading S., when a pick-up truck approached . Rolling down the window, he smiled and asked if we needed any help. As we explained our mission, he told us he lived on the Charlie Kurtz place. Of course, Mother knew Charlie Kurtz, well. She had gone to school with him. It was a pleasure to talk with Van Lawson and to see what an interest a local person had in the history of his community.

There were so many neighbors and friends that Catherine remembers, many of whom have remained friends over all the years. There were the Trents and their children; Fred, Maude, Merle, Troy, Ray, Benny and Ethel Ruth. There were the Blantons, the Spilkers, the Hadleys, the Washburns, Carters, Dooleys, Paces, Bensons, Osborns, the Scotts and the Kurtzs, just to name a few. I could not write fast enough to catch all the names! The children in the area didn't have to look far for something to do. The rolling hills and ravines, the woods and meandering streams supplied all that is necessary for children of any era to enjoy!

Catherine remembers swimming in the creek with Margaret Kurtz, and the adventures with the Trent children were endless.

Catherine remembers that being a girl, sandwiched between two brothers, all close in age, was a never ending adventure! Her older brother, Ledner, was a leader and very outgoing. Her younger brother, Robert, was the engineer of the family... always taking things apart, building and experimenting. Robert had an old buggy chassis, and by tying a rope to the axle, he could sit on the chassis and steer. All he needed was a hill for a test drive. With Catherine's help, he got all lined up at the top of a hill. The hill is on today's Co. Rd. 350 N., just off S.R. 75. With only a little urging, Catherine jumped on. The chassis picked up considerable speed, as any vehicle with

no brakes would do! However, Robert was in firm control, and their chariot was nearing the bottom of the hill, when Catherine saw it... a long black snake lying across the middle of the road! She shut her eyes. She didn't know if they ran over it or not, for as soon as they slowed down enough, she jumped off, grabbed up her skirt and ran for home, leaving Robert to fend for himself!

As we drove, Catherine recounted about the summer her father had an extra job. He worked for the county, grading the gravel (probably mostly dirt) roads, using a large, heavy drag pulled by 3 work horses. This helped to keep the roads smoothed out for travel. It was a hot and hard job, for the horses and for her father. He had a certain route and by noon time, he would be at the Washburn farm, which sits at the corner of today's Co. Rd. 200 N. and S.R. 75 . Here, her father would water and feed the horses. Catherine and her family would meet her father there and bring him his noon dinner.

Catherine's family attended the North Salem Methodist Church. Reuben Claypool was the first minister when the church was organized about 1833. Catherine was about 9 when she and her family started attending this church. It was, then, a wooden

North Salem United Methodist Church.

structure located on today's S.R. 75, near
Martins Green House. As they rode to
and from church, she recalls a spring along
the road(S.R. 75), where her father would
stop to let all the children get a drink.
In 1923, the present Methodist Church was
built. During the construction, Catherine
remembers that the congregation met in
the movie house, located on the south side
of the main St. Catherine and her friends
now enjoy the pancake breakfast that is
served in the Methodist Church on Labor
Day weekend during North Salem's Old
Fashioned Days!

North Salem was laid out in 1835 by
David Claypool, Sr., John S. Woodward
and John Claypool. After the construction
of the I.D.& S. Railroad (Indianapolis,
Decatur & Southern) on the southeast

side of town in 1880, North Salem experienced its greatest period of prosperity and development.
This growth is apparent, today, by the large collection a late 19th Century buildings. The business district is surrounded by, primarily, Queen Ann houses, an

Downtown North Salem

impressive example of a late 19th Century railroad town. The large, gracious homes, the winding streets, lovely churches and the picturesque downtown area , with its antique shops, quaint soda shoppe and eateries, along with the relaxed atmosphere, make North Salem an Indiana treasure.

The first school in North Salem was held in a house about 1/2 mile southeast of town in about 1829. It was taught by Wm Dewitt, who lived to be 115. This tiny school must have been a sharp contrast to the impressive North Salem Elementary School of today, which instructs and cultivates the children of Eel River and Union Town-

ships. These two townships, along with Middle Township now form the North West Hendricks School Corporation. The Jr. and Sr. High students attend the spacious Tri-West Jr. Sr. High School Campus, located in Lizton, on S.R. 39, just south of U.S. 136.

When Catherine was 13, her youngest

New Winchester, Catherine's and Ledner's, combined classes, around 1919

New Winchester school hack, early 1900's.. Source: Mary Jeanette Winkleman

brother, Donald Verne, was born. This would complete their family of 3 boys and 2 girls. On that cold, snowy January day in 1924, Doc Wisehart had been summoned. He got nearly to the house, but his car could not make it up the last hill, which is on today's Co. Rd. 625. He grabbed his black medical bag and walked the rest of the way, making it in time to bring Don into the world.

Doc Wisehart had two children. His son, Bob was an eye Dr. in Lebanon for years, and his daughter , Louise, gave violin lessons to Catherine.

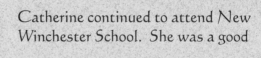

New Winchester class reunion of 1928 and 29 at Catherine's home.

Catherine continued to attend New Winchester School. She was a good

student and won a Spelling Contest in the
7th/8th Grade. Her teacher was Mable
Joseph, and she awarded Catherine a copy
of Kilmeny of the Orchard, a book which
she still treasures. The children of that
area were taken to and from school in a
school hack. One morning, as the horse
was pulling the hack, a wheel fell off,
tipping the hack. This was on today's Co.
Rd. 200 E and St. Rd. 75. The children
waited beside the road while the repairs
were made. Catherine says they got a
"real" school bus about her first year of
high school The classes of 1928 and 1929
still get together for a reunion each summer.
Keeping in touch with family was very
important, so they made frequent trips to
Noblesville, Cicero, Lapel and Anderson
to visit their grandparents, aunts and uncles
and cousins. When they passed through
Lebanon, Catherine's father would often
stop at the drug store, which was then on
the corner of Noble St. and S.R. 39.

Ethel and Vern in the touring car with Ledner,
Robert, Laurabel and Catherine, about 1919.

The family would go in, sit sown and enjoy a drink and, maybe, a piece of pie. Catherine's father always ordered a Coca-Cola. Catherine was about 10, and she decided that she would order a Coca-Cola, too. She smiled as the lady brought 2 Coca-Colas in fancy glasses with red striped paper straws. She took a big sip... her eyes watered... there must be some mistake, she thought. She looked at her father. He smiled as he sipped his drink. Catherine drank hers, for she knew her father would not allow her to waste it, but it was awhile before she developed the acquired taste for Coke! Catherine's mother never drank Coca-Cola or any other "pop". She considered it to be, at the least, unnecessary and unhealthy, and at the most, bordering on sinful! Oh yes, Cokes cost a nickel...

In North Salem, nearly every Saturday evening in the summertime, there was a band concert. A wooden platform would be set up in the intersection, and local musicians would play, much to the enjoy-ment of crowds of people who came from all over the area. Catherine's parents did not attend the concerts, but Catherine loved them. She would catch a ride with her friends, the Trents. They all enjoyed an evening of music and dancing in the streets, and ice cream was to be had for 5 cents!

As we completed our tour through Catherine Genevieve's memory, we enjoyed lunch in Liz's Cafe, next to the Red Dog Tavern. It was cozy and full of

Red Dog Tavern

the good smells you expect in a small cafe. The local people sat, talking, eating, enjoying the good home cooking, the fresh brewed coffee and tea. Country music played softly in the background, and the rain continued to drizzle outside.

We smiled as we left...Life was very good for Catherine Genevieve, growing up in the heartland of Indiana.....

Life is still very good!

Now, let bring you up to date on Catherine and her family...

After Catherine graduated in 1929, she worked and lived in Indianapolis, in the Lockerby area. She worked at the Glove Factory. On a blind date, arranged by a co-worker, she met Robert Coleman, who worked at Real Silk, on North Park Ave. The nation was deep in depression, but both these young people had been raised in the country by kind and loving, down to earth families who instilled in them a never give up attitude and a faith and optimism, sprinkled with a sense of humor that continues to influence their children, grandchildren and great-grandchildren!

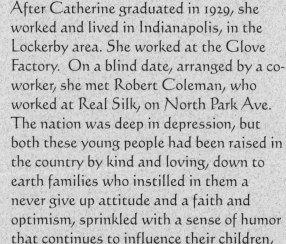

Catherine Genevieve Wolfe) Coleman   *Robert William Coleman*

After Ledner and Catherine graduated from New Winchester, her parents moved to the Pittsboro area, where Robert, Laurabel and Donald all finished high school. Catherine's parents semi-retired in Pittsboro. Many of you will remember Verne and Ethel Wolfe living, until their deaths, in the home just west of the Methodist Church on U.S. 136.

Don, Laurabel, Robert, Catherine and Ledner, 1976

Ledner married Edna Mae Rutledge. They spent their lives on a farm in Hendricks Co. They had 5 children: Mary, Jean, Kay, Donna and Allen. Catherine married Robert Coleman. They lived on a grain and dairy farm in Hendricks Co.. They raised two children: Kenneth and Susan. Catherine still resides in Hendricks Co. Robert married Wilma Fulk. They raised 4 children: Carl, Tom, Roy and Betty. They

lived in Boone Co., then moved to Florida, where they reside today.

Laurabel married Clarence Pruitt⁻. They had 3 children: Carol, Jim and Bob. They lived in Speedway, then settled in Hendricks Co., where Laurabel lives today.

Don married Myrtle Clark⁻. They raised 7 children: Jerry, David⁻, Ed, Reta, Janet, Alice and Amy. They farmed in Hendricks Co. Today, Don and his wife, Mary, reside in Boone Co.

REMEMBER...LIFE IS FULL OF UNEXPECTED ADVENTURES... ENJOY YOURS!

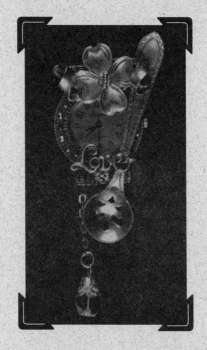

MEET CATHERINE Genevieve (WOLFE) COLEMAN TODAY

Catherine has lived nearly all her adult life in Hendricks County, Indiana. She has a great interest in the community and is an active, dedicated member of her Pittsboro United Methodist church family.

She enjoyed working for several years in Indianapolis, however, her true calling was being a farm wife and mother.

She was married to Robert William Coleman for 30 years, and together they raised a son and a daughter and operated a grain and dairy farm.

Today Catherine still lives in Hendricks County. Her cozy bungalow with its flower garden remain the favorite family gathering place for every holiday, spilling onto the front porch for the 4th of July.... I think I can smell that apple pie, now...

Our Family Stories

Our Family Stories

Our Family Stories

Our Family Stories

Our Family Stories

Our Family Stories

Our Family Stories

_____

_____

_____

_____

_____

_____

_____

_____

_____

_____

_____

_____

_____

_____

_____

_____

_____

_____

_____

_____

_____

Our Family Stories